PHANTOMS
Forever

Osprey Colour Series

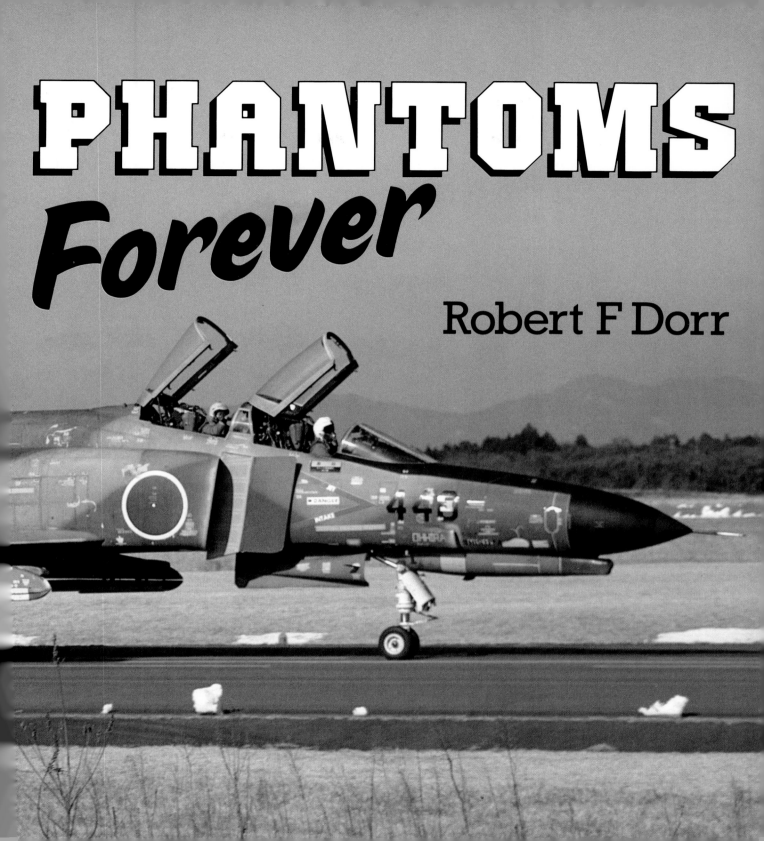

PHANTOMS
Forever

Robert F Dorr

Published in 1987 by Osprey Publishing Limited
27A Floral Street, London WC2E 9DP
Member company of the George Philip Group

British Library Cataloguing in Publication Data

Dorr, Robert F.
    Phantoms forever.—(Osprey colour series)
    1. Phantom (Fighter plane)—History—Pictorial works
    I. Title
    623.74'64   UG1242.S5

ISBN 0-85045-742-4

Editor Dennis Baldry
Designed by David Tarbutt
Printed in Hong Kong

Front cover A neat four-ship of Taegu-based F-
4E Phantoms in service with the Republic of
Korea Air Force (ROKAF) wearing standardized
Compass Ghost II low-visibility warpaint. South
Korea received the first of 41 F-4Es (37 plus 4
recent attrition replacements from US stocks) in
1977 to supplement its existing force of 36 F-4D
models. To preserve security, the ROKAF is
reluctant to release any specific information; the
'number plate' of this particular squadron is
unknown to the author at the time of writing
[*ROKAF*]

Title pages The 5201st and final Phantom built
came not from James S McDonnell's once-
unknown firm in midwest cowtown but from the
Mitsubishi factory in Nagoya, Japan, the only
foreign builder. This F-4EJ Phantom (17-8440)
was delivered to the Komatsu-based 303rd Fighter
Squadron of the Japan Air Self-Defence Force on
21 May 1981 and later transferred to the 302nd
squadron at the same base. Seen visiting Hyaku-ri
in February 1984, the Phantom temporarily wears
a disruptive camouflage scheme used for tactical
exercises
[*Toshiki Kudo*]

'*We Bad*,' proclaim cartoon characters Heckle and
Jeckle, on the nose of F-4C Phantom 63-7412 of
the 191st Fighter-Interceptor Group, Michigan
Air National Guard, seen away from its Selfridge
home and visiting Tyndall AFB, Florida on 10
August 1984. Skipper of the group, also known as
the Six Pack, Col Dave Arendts decided he
wanted colourful figures on his airplanes and
many, like these, were painted by
Guardsman/artist Bill Quan with permission from
the copyright holders. In 1986, Arendts' Six Pack
began converting from the F-4C to F-4D model
[*H J van Broekhuizen*]

For a generation, Phantoms have risen from land and sea to take command of the air. The McDonnell F-4 Phantom II is, simply, the most important and best-known fighter aircraft of the second half of the twentieth century. Phantoms will still be flying long after the century is finished, and will probably serve in more countries than the thirteen which have employed the airplane already. In its day, the Phantom was the standard against which all other fighters were measured, and it is surprising how true this remains, even now.

On the pages which follow are Phantoms in full afterburner, Phantoms wearing the rising sun of Japan, Phantoms marked with MiG kills, Phantoms, Phantoms, Phantoms. None of these colour pictures have ever been published before.

Together, the pictures in this volume form a celebration of a widely-appreciated airplane which is still making history and will continue to be celebrated for years to come.

Enjoy. Phantoms no longer roll off anyone's production line, but they will be flying for a long time to come. They are always a sight to behold, and on the pages which follow an attempt has been made to capture some of that sight, to put it on paper, and to keep it for those who will be asking about the F-4 Phantom II years in the future. For assembling this archive of colour views, no better reason need be enunciated. Enjoy them.

Robert F Dorr
London, September 1986

Robert F Dorr is the author of *McDonnell Douglas F-4 Phantom II* in the Osprey Air Combat series. Bob is continuing his efforts to collect a colour slide of every Phantom built, and has gotten coverage on 2700 of the 5201 airframes in the series. Bob is an established aviation historian and writer. His fascination for McDonnell fighters is reflected in his latest volume in the Osprey Air Combat series on the F-101 Voodoo, released in March 1987.

This volume takes a new approach in the Osprey Colour Series in bringing together the work of many fine photographers. *Phantoms Forever* would not have been possible without the help of Charles W Arrington, Flight Lieutenant Ian Black, Robert L Burns, Flight Lieutenant Tristram J Carter, Dr Joseph G Handelman, Colonel G F Robert Hanke, Major James Rotramel, Captain Keith Svendson and Douglas R Tachauer. Additional material came from photographers who are credited individually. Bob Dorr and editor Dennis Baldry assembled pictures and text in what Bob calls not a history but a 'celebration.'

After four years in the West End of London with his wife, Young Soon and two boys, Bobbie and Jerry, 47-year-old Bob Dorr recently returned to Washington, DC in his 'other life' as a diplomat with the US Department of State. Bob Dorr is a member of the Tailhook Association and the Red River Valley Fighter Pilots Association, and expects to maintain his lifelong interest in the Phantom.

Phantoms Forever is dedicated to Major Robert A Lodge, who got three MiGs and left a tradition of leadership before being shot down by a MiG-19 on 10 May 1972.

From Duluth, from Fresno, from Fargo . . . Air Guardsmen line up at Andrews AFB, Maryland on 1 March 1986, heading for Ramstein AB, Germany, to relieve the regular air force's F-4E-equipped 86th Tactical Fighter Wing so it can convert to the F-16 Fighting Falcon. F-4D Phantom (66-7478) of 119th Fighter-Interceptor Group, North Dakota Air National Guard, is in foreground
[*Joseph G Handelman*]

Contents

In the Navy

In disruptive camouflage scheme devised by artist
Keith Ferris, F-4J of the 'Be-devilers' of squadron
VF-74 sits on the steam catapult of USS *Forrestal*
(CV-59) in the Atlantic on 2 August 1977. Green-
jacketed launch crew are part of the precision
choreography which transforms a dangerous
carrier deck into a functioning environment
[*Robert L Burns*]

Above left Ferris camouflage blends into the background sky as F-4J of VF-74 hurls aloft from *Forrestal*'s deck on 2 August 1977. Under Commander Julian Lake, the squadron was one of the first to operate Phantoms in the early 1960s. Now, the 'Be-devilers' fly the Grumman F-14A Tomcat
[*Robert L Burns*]

Left F-4J Phantom of the 'Sluggers' of VF-103 in new, low-visibility paint scheme at NAS Oceana, Virginia in August 1981. In-flight refuelling probe, raised from its normal position, may be responding to some gesture from observers. Located at Virginia Beach, the Oceana air station is home for US Navy fighter aviation on the east coast while this squadron is traditionally associated with USS *Saratoga* (CV-60)
[*James Rotramel*]

F-4J Phantom 155529 of VF-171 poses at Key West in November 1981
[*James Rotramel*]

Preceding pages, this page, and overleaf
'People power' exertion by deck crewmen
positioning F-4J Phantom (153784), coded AA-
200, of USS *Forrestal*'s Be-Devilers heads up a
half-dozen scenes from Bob Burns' examination of
the carrier's work-ups on 2 August 1977. AD-204
is another F-4J Phantom (157287) of VF-74 (p. 16,
bottom left). A US Navy study confirmed that
experienced Phantom pilots reacted with greater
apprehension to carrier deck landings than to
battle with North Vietnamese MiGs
[*Robert L Burns*]

Bright red panels and tail emblem mark the Strike Test Directorate (STD) at NATC Patuxent River, or 'Pax,' in the Maryland tidewater where naval aviators test airframes, equipment and themselves. F-4J Phantom (153839) is trailing its parabrake · after landing at Pax on 6 November 1978 (above), while its companion 153768 (right) differs in having the rear-fin radar warning and homing system (RHAWS) antenna found since the late 1960s on most Phantoms except reconnaissance models
[*Robert L Burns*]

F-4B Phantom (152269), side number ND-102, a distant visitor from the 'Devil's Disciples' of Reserve squadron VF-301 at NAS Miramar near San Diego, California, pauses at Andrews AFB, Maryland on 10 August 1974. Reservist pilots and radar intercept officers on Navy Phantoms were fully carrier- and combat-qualified and provided a powerful backup to regular aircrews in the Fleet [*Joseph G Handelman*]

F-4B Phantom (150993) of the Naval Missile
Center at Point Mugu, California captured by
dentist/photographer Joe Handelman at Andrews
AFB, Maryland on 24 February 1972, at a time
when US warplanes were about to return to
North Vietnam. Inboard tank with NMC logo is a
travel pod, for luggage
[Joseph G Handelman]

By thirteen years later, as a precaution against visual and infrared sighting by latter-day enemies, aircraft markings had become so toned-down that only the black numeral 7 was easily readable on this NMC Point Mugu F-4S Phantom on 26 October 1985. Point Mugu is the US Navy's principal testing ground for its air-to-air and air-to-surface weaponry
[*Robert L Burns*]

Marine machines

The 'Gray Ghosts' of VMFA-531 were the first
Marines to operate the McDonnell fighter (in June
1962) and first to take it into combat (in April
1965). During the latter month at Da Nang AB,
South Vietnam, F-4B Phantom (151443), side
number EC-9, sports the squadron's death's head
(left). Same time, same place, F-4B Phantom
(151483), coded EC-4 (above) carries six Zuni
rocket pods inboard and twelve Mk 82 500-lb
(227-kg) bombs outboard—but it wouldn't carry
this load very far! Initially, the defence of airfields
was given as the reason for moving Marine F-4Bs
into the combat zone. Later they went north
[*G F Robert Hanke*]

The brightest-painted Phantoms ever, the 'Hell's Angels' of Reserve squadron VMFA-321 were literally star-spangled in April 1975 when F-4B airplane (151002), side number MG-7 operated from Andrews AFB. *Zero Zero Two* had earlier served as an Air Force developmental ship with serial 62-12185. Later, it became one of 228 B models rebuilt with improved systems and redesignated F-4N.
[*Joseph G Handelman*]

The 'Sharpshooters' of VMFAT-101 at MCAS
Yuma, Arizona were the Marine Corps' sole
replacement training unit, operating F-4N
Phantom (152230), coded SH-26, in February
1976
[*James Rotramel*]

Above left F-4N Phantom (150456), side number MG-4, at Andrews AFB in May 1978, was still an F-4B model when it shot down a MiG-17 while serving with the 'Screaming Eagles' of VF-51 on 6 May 1972
[*Joseph G Handelman*]

Left Fourth and final paint scheme for VMFA-321 'Hells Angels' adorns F-4S Phantom (153860), coded MG-10, visiting NAS Oceana, Virginia on 19 April 1986. 248 airframes were converted from F-4J to F-4S with addition of leading-edge manoeuvre slats, advanced avionics, and other improvements
[*Joseph G Handelman*]

Above In a third variation of VMFA-321 colours, F-4N Phantom (150536), coded MG-10, pushes its own braking parachute, taxying in, in May 1980. Fin cap of this Hell's Angels reveals the final of several configurations which changed as additional radar warning receivers were added to Navy/Marine airplanes
[*James Rotramel*]

Overleaf F-4N Phantom (151415), coded MA-11, of Dallas-based Reserve squadron VMFA-112 on approach to MCAS El Toro, California in April 1983. Even this late, the McDonnell machine was still emitting telltale exhaust. The F-4S model finally introduced smokeless engines
[*Douglas R Tachauer*]

It's actually an F-4N, as the fin cap contours
reveal, but this 'gate guard' Phantom (152270),
coded DW-1, is supposed to represent an F-4B of
the 'Thunderbolts' of VMFA-251. Location is the
Marine Corps' final Phantom base, MCAS
Beaufort, South Carolina, on 14 July 1986
[*Joseph G Handelman*]

The last Phantom cruise by the 'Death Rattlers' of VMFA-323 was a Westpac journey in October 1979 aboard USS *Coral Sea* (CV-43). When the Snakes next embarked on *Coral Maru* in April 1986, they were flying the F/A-18A Hornet in combat against Libya. Preceding both events, basking in the burn of sun in a day when aircraft markings still evoked interest, F-4N Phantom (150485), side number WS-10, of the El Toro-based squadron paused in its travels at Andrews AFB on 29 September 1974. The venom of the rattlesnake had been dispensed liberally in Vietnam in yet an earlier era, when VMFA-323 flew more than a hundred thousand combat sorties [*Joseph G Handelman*]

Preceding page and overleaf Marine Corps aviation is constituted in three Marine Aircraft Wings, corresponding to the three ground combat divisions they support, located on the east coast, west coast and in Japan. When Brigadier General Mike Sullivan, exec of the 2nd MAW on the east coast, recently logged his 5000th flying hour in a Phantom, his feat simply underscored the long association of the Corps with the airplane. In 1986, Major Michael Humberd, also located at Beaufort or 'Phantom Town,' became the fourth Marine to chalk up 4000 hours in the type. Beaufort will be the last base for the Corps' Phantoms and the DR-coded 'Checkerboards' of VMFA-312 will be the final squadron, finally converting to the F/A-18A Hornet in 1989. Meanwhile, the squadron will continue to operate F-4S airplanes like 155764, DR-14; 157268, DR-09; 155830, DR-04; 155517, DR-10 and 158374, DR-12
[*Joseph G Handelman*]

Left Only 46 examples of the Marine Corps' RF-4B reconnaissance Phantom were delivered. They served for so long, in so many places, that each machine ended up being internally slightly different from each of the others. Four were lost in combat in Vietnam. Initially, each Marine Air Wing had its own composite recce squadron operating the RF-4B, these being VMCJ-1 at Iwakuni, Japan; VMCJ-2 at Cherry Point, North Carolina, and VMCJ-3 at El Toro. RF-4B Phantom (157347), coded CY-4, of the 'Playboys' of VMCJ-2, users of the magazine's famous rabbit, visits Andrews AFB in July 1974. In September 1975, all RF-4B operations were consolidated in a single squadron, VMFP-3, the 'Eyes of the Corps,' located at El Toro [*Joseph G Handelman*]

In the early Phantom era, the 'Gray Ghosts' of VMFA-531 may have been the world's premier fighter squadron. The Marines deployed to Key West in late 1962 to look across 90 miles of water at Castro's MiG-17s during the Cuban Missile Crisis. In June 1964, the squadron began a Westpac deployment which ended not with the usual joyous return home but, instead, with its arrival in a new war nine months later in April 1965. The first Westpac deployment by Phantoms saw the F-4Bs in 'clean' condition except for wingtanks (page 43). They made several refuellings en route from KC-130F Hercules tankers, including this one between Midway and NAF Atsugi, Japan on 28 June 1964 (page 41). Somewhere out in those vast Pacific reaches, F-4B Phantom (150407), coded EC-17, made a pretty picture against the clouds (page 39). Another 39

squadron jet (151456), side number EC-7, passes over Japan's Mount Fuji (page 42) en route to the battle zone

Captain G F Robert Hanke (left) and Captain Edward Janz were two of the VMFA-531 front-seat pilots who began combat operations from Da Nang in April 1965 (right). Hanke had been one of the first Marines to log 1000 Phantom hours. Their machine carries AIM-7 Sparrows, 500-lb (227-kg) bombs and Zuni rocket packs. On a typical combat mission from Da Nang (above), airplane in foreground (151448) totes bombs while its partner carries Zunis
[G F Robert Hanke]

Air Force and Air Guard

High over the NATO front, pilot in red-trimmed helmet leads a two-ship formation from the 23rd Tactical Fighter Squadron, 52nd Tactical Fighter Wind based at Spangdahlem AB, Germany in May 1982. More recently, helmets have become camouflaged and the 52 TFW has converted to the F-16A Fighting Falcon. The number-two machine in this patrol (above) is F-4D Phantom (66-8735), tailcode SP. The F-4D model was built to give the Air Force a fighter-bomber suited for its own needs, one not solely a derivative of a Navy design. 71 of them, like this one, were equipped with AN/ARN-92 LORAN navigation gear for Southeast Asia operations, resulting in a distinctive 'towel rack' antenna on the spine of the aircraft
[*James Rotramel*]

Left Continuing our Spangdahlem mission not far from the watching Russians, LORAN-equipped F-4D Phantom (66-8735), coded SP, of the 52nd TFW mates on a KC-135 tanker high over Germany
[*James Rotramel*]

Above F-4C Phantoms (foreground, 64-0780), coded HF, of the 113th TFS, Indiana Air National Guard, at Terre Haute in April 1980. The aircraft up front carries Sidewinder infrared heat-seaking missiles and is painted with three F-15 Eagle kills, reflecting friendly skirmishes
[*James Rotramel*]

With Major Jim Walsh and Captain Ron Mercer as its crew, RF-4C Phantom (65-0841), callsign SKATE 41, of the 165th TRS/123rd TRW, Kentucky Air National Guard, banks gently at 10,000 ft (3,050 m) over Illinois in April 1984. Reconnaissance Phantoms date to 1963, and 503 airframes in the RF-4C series were built, many lost in Vietnam. The Louisville-based Kentucky Guardsmen, under Colonel Joseph L Kottak, once flew the RF-101H Voodoo. In 1987, theirs was one of six ANG recce squadrons, all flying the RF-4C
[*Douglas R Tachauer*]

Before the time of Col Arendts' cartoon characters on 15 September 1979, F-4C Phantom (63-7536) of Selfridge-based 191st FIG, Michigan Air National Guard, taxies in
[*James Rotramel*]

Overleaf Previously seen at the beginning of this book, Heckle and Jeckel continue their 24 October 1984 sortie on the nose of Michigan ANG's 63-7412
[*H J van Broekhuizen*]

Preceding pages Piloted by Colonel John Cook, F-4C Phantom (63-7428) in the rainbow colours of the 136th FIS/107th FIG, New York Air National Guard—one of the oldest in inventory—poses at 16,000 ft (4,877 m) over Lake Ontario for the elder of Canada's intrepid Tachauer brothers in November 1983. The Niagara Falls ANG squadron was scheduled to convert to the F-15A Eagle in 1987. Defence of North America has been largely the charge of Air Guardsmen who bolster the interceptor strength of TAC's recently-formed First Air Force
[*Douglas R Tachauer*]

The location is linked in American minds to that most peculiar of customs, the honeymoon, but Niagara Falls is also home for triple MiG killer (64-0660) making a stopover at Dayton, Ohio in July 1985 (above) and for similar F-4C Phantom (64-0661) depicted at home in July 1984
[*Douglas R Tachauer*]

(**Above left**) F-4E Phantom (67-0314), coded GA, of the 35th Tactical Fighter Wing taxies at George AFB near Victorville, California in October 1981. The T.O.114 camouflage seems unsuited to the desert climate of the American Southwest but, unlike Israel, the US never developed a tropical paint scheme. F-4E was the most numerous Phantom, no fewer than 1397 having been manufactured
[*Douglas R Tachauer*]

Left North of the border, CFB Trenton is often home to US-Canadian joint exercises. F-4C Phantom (64-780), tail-code HF, drops in during August 1984, as an envoy of the 113th TFS/181st TFG, Indiana Air National Guard, one of two Phantom units from the Hoosier state, headquartered at Terre Haute
[*Douglas R Tachauer*]

Above First Air National Guard unit to employ the E model Phantom is the SL-coded (for St Louis) 110th TFS/131st TFW, representing the proud state of Missouri. The squadron also introduced a new, one-piece, bird-resistant windshield. F-4E Phantom (69-7267), with toned-down USAF insignia, lizard-green 'Europe One' camouflage and shark's teeth, taxies on a visit to London, Ontario International Airport in June 1986
[*Douglas R Tachauer*]

F-4C Phantom (63-7615), with FW code, belonged to the 163rd TFS/122nd TFW, the other Indiana ANG squadron, located at Fort Wayne. Phantom is depicted in July 1982 [*Douglas R Tachauer*]

'Egypt One' is the misleading term given to the
new air defense gray colouration being worn by
Air Guard fighters. The 121st TFS/113rd TFW,
District of Columbia Air National Guard operated
the F-86E, F-100D and F-105D before acquiring
a logical DC tailcode for the F-4D Phantoms
which now occupy its corner of Andrews AFB.
This one (66-7688), on 15 March 1986, has an
incorrect serial number presentation on the tail
[*Joseph G Handelman*]

Earlier and better-known air defense gray paint
job is seen on F-4C Phantom (63-7420) of the 111
FIS, Texas Air Guard, commanded by Lt Col.
'Mo' Udell, at Ellington AFB, Texas on 5 August
1983
[*James Rotramel*]

By the time the California Air National Guard folks belatedly laid hands on Phantoms at March AFB near Riverside, gray was about to become good and T.O. 114 camouflage was about to become as trendy as the Montgolfier brothers. Result: the colour combination seen here, including black national insignia and blue-white fin flash, was short-lived and very rare. F-4C Phantom (63-7545) is seen in April 1983. Yellow strips on fuselage and vertical tail are formation trip lights, added to most Phantoms in the late 1960s and now *de regueur* for Eagles and Hornets [*Douglas R Tachauer*]

61

They sit in tandem, Jim. At the same Arizona locale (as pictured below), F-4C Phantom (63-7411) coded LA of the 550th Tactical Fighter Training Squadron burned rubber in December 1975 for the camera of Lieutenant Rotramel who was, himself, about to become weapons systems officer on the F-111. Luke AFB, near Glendale, was for many years the place where Phantom crews earned their combat-ready status. Their wing commander was Brig Gen Fred A Haeffner, who got one MiG and another 'probable' during the difference of opinion in Southeast Asia [*James Rotramel*]

'If it quacks. . .' It looks like any old American
Phantom. It even wears factory-fresh but
erroneous national insignia, lacking blue bars
around the rectangular fields, in which McDonnell
delivered hundreds of Phantoms and Eagles. Not
American at all, 75-0418 is an Israeli Defence
Force/Air Force (IDF/AF) RF-4E photo-recce
machine in Compass Ghost gray, pausing at Luke
AFB, Arizona on 10 March 1977 for installation
of avionics before being delivered to Israel.
Israel's were the only recce Phantoms to carry
Sidewinder missiles on operational missions
[*Robert C Bush*]

Left At 33,000 ft (10,060 m) over the peaceful
farms and fields of Ohio, four Air Reserve crews
fly bomb-laden Phantoms painted lizard green for
warfare in Europe. The DO tailcode (for Dayton,
Ohio) signifies the 89th TFS/906th TFG and the
closest airplane in this July 1985 formation is F-
4D Phantom (66-7650). Two F-4Ds carry
conventional M117 500-lb (227-kg) bombs while
two carry AGM-65E laser Maverick missiles.
Overleaf, 66-7650 with red trim and tail
maintains a steady position against a deep blue sky
[*Douglas R Tachauer*]

65

Above Nearby Las Vegas may be better known for showgirls, one-armed bandits and blackjack tables, but Nellis AFB is fighter country. F-4E Phantom (67-0270), coded WA, of the 414th Fighter Weapons Squadron, 57th Fighter Weapons Wing under Colonel William L. Strand, carrying simulated Sidewinder electronic scoring devices, enjoys Nellis's sunshine in February 1976. The absence of a red star on the splitter vane indicates that no one had noticed at the time, but on 29 July 1972, while attached to the 4th/TFS/366th TFW and operating out of Da Nang, crewed by Lt Col Gene E Taft and Captain Stanley M Imaye, this very Phantom with the callsign PISTOL 01 used an AIM-7E-2 Sparrow missile to blast a MiG-21 out of North Vietnamese skies
[*James Rotramel*]

Right First man to fly faster than sound, Colonel Charles E Yeager commanded the 4th Tactical Fighter Wing in 1968 when the wing was rushed from Seymour Johnson AFB, North Carolina to Korea during the *Pueblo* crisis. Following his return, Yeager's personal aircraft, F-4D Phantom (66-7678), coded SA, paused at Andrews AFB, Maryland. Indian head making up part of the colourful fin cap is a traditional emblem of the 4th TFW
[*Joseph G Handelman*]

Overleaf YF-4E Phantom (65-0713) was built as an F-4D and converted to E model configuration. On 11 April 1984, in its role as a test ship for the 6512nd TS/6510th TW, Air Force Flight Test Center (AFFTC), Edwards AFB, California, the YF-4E was being wrung out in brilliant sunshine over Rodgers Dry Lake
[*Keith Svendson*]

Left Air Force flight engineer Keith Svendson, who has flown in everything up through the cranked-wing F-16XL Fighting Falcon, was up over Edwards on 3 September 1984 when his viewfinder located the test centre's red and white recce bird. RF-4C Phantom (63-7744), with Edwards' ED tailcode, is one of several machines in the AFFTC test stable
[*Keith Svendson*]

Preceding pages Another view of the 11 April 1984 sortie by YF-4E Phantom (65-0713), a standard bearer at Edwards for many years. The ED code is recent, but the shark's teeth have been on and off the tailplane several times during its long tenure in the flight test centre
[*Keith Svendson*]

Above Twelve years before the flight depicted in the previous photo, Edwards-based YF-4E Phantom (65-0713) pauses at MCAS Yuma, Arizona on 18 December 1972. The 'spook' on the tail is an inseparable part of the Phantom story
[*Lars G Soldeus*]

Above and preceding pages Piloted by Captain Guy Walsh and used as a chase plane for the ALCM (air-launched cruise missile), F-4C Phantom (63-7407), coded ED, is the oldest Phantom in service anywhere but had been recently repainted before this 3 May 1985 sortie. Purpose of 'Europe One' camouflage on a California test ship is unclear but Phantoms have now been flying at Edwards for a quarter-century [*Keith Svendson*]

Under MiG killer Colonel Fred A Haeffner, the 58th TFTW at Luke AFB, Arizona wore training bands and other extraordinary markings during the 1975–76 period, including:

—standard T.O.114 camouflage on 63-7598 in July 1975 (above), 63-7556 in August 1975 (page 80), 63-7631 in June 1976 (page 81), 64-0820 in December 1975 (page 82), and 64-0899 in March 1976 (page 83).

—red and white bands for the 550th TFTS commander's aircraft (63-7550) in February 1976 at the first Red Flag exercise.

—black and white bands and multi-squadron tail stripes for Haeffner's wing commander's aircraft (63-7584), nicknamed *Adidas*, in March 1976 (page 84).

Two-tone gray Ferris disruptive camouflage on 63-7598 in July 1976 (page 86).

—yellow band on the 426th TFTS commander's aircraft in March 1976 (page 87).

[*James Rotramel*]

Wearing the GA tailcode of the 35th Tactical
Fighter Wing at George AFB, California, the F-
4E Phantom makes a pretty picture over the
southwest desert in May 1974
[*James Rotramel*]

Overleaf Though it wears two red stars on its
splitter plate, this Phantom is understood to be
credited only with the MiG-21 downed using an
AIM-9 Sidewinder missile on 31 May 1972 by the
13th TFS/432nd TRW crew of Captain Bruce G

Leonard, Jr and Captain Jeffrey S Feinstein,
callsign GOPHER 03. Feinstein went on to
become the fifth and final American ace of the air
war against North Vietnam. F-4E Phantom (68-
338), with SL code, of the 110th TFS/131st
TFW, Missouri ANG, makes a visit to Williams
AFB, Arizona on 12 October 1985
[*Douglas E Slowiak*]

Left F-4G Wild Weasel (69-7287), coded WW, of the 563rd TFS/37th TFW lifts off from George AFB, California in August 1981. 116 F-4Es were converted to F-4G standard for the electronic warfare role and more may follow [*James Rotramel*]

F-4C Phantom (64-829) was the personal mount of Colonel Robin Olds, commander of the 8th TFW 'Wolfpack,' and accounted for two of Olds' four MiG kills. Still wearing 'Europe One' camouflage and the SA tailcode (for San Antonio) of the Kelly Field-based 182nd TFS/149th TFG, Texas Air National Guard, old Eight Two Niner had arrived in Dayton, Ohio in May 1986 to be put on display at the US Air Force Museum [*David W Menard*]

Left The red star adorning F-4D Phantom (66-7661) on 15 March 1986 is thought to be the personal tally of a pilot, since the airframe is not known to have been credited with a MiG kill. Six Six One belongs to the 121st TFS/113th TFW, District of Columbia Air National Guard, based at Andrews AFB, Maryland
[*Joseph G Handelman*]

Above In 1967, camouflage was new, tailcodes were new, and the 'Gunfighters' of the 389th TFS/366th TFW were caught up in the frenetic Rolling Thunder campaign against North Vietnam. Before the introduction of formation light strips and other features from a later period, F-4C Phantom (64-0797), with a one-off AH tailcode, taxies at Da Nang AB, South Vietnam
[*Charles W Arrington*]

Left F-4C Phantom of the 12th Tactical Fighter Wing at Cam Ranh Bay AB, South Vietnam in September 1967. Only a careful look at a map discloses that targets in North Vietnam were closer to Thai airbases than to Cam Ranh Bay, which was nevertheless a masterpiece of American engineering, built on tidal landfill where nothing had existed before. Today, the airfield is home for Soviet MiG-23 *Flogger F* fighters
[*Norm Malayney*]

Above At Saigon's Tan Son Nhut airbase, a pair of RF-4C Phantoms of Brig Gen Robert J Holbury's 460th Tactical Reconnaissance Wing sit in revetments on 19 February 1968. Airplane closest to camera appears to have been a victim of one of the many Viet Cong mortar attacks on the airfield
[*Nicholas M Williams*]

Above The blue and red bands on the fuselage identify F-4D Phantom (66-7554), coded OY, as a 555th TFS/432nd TRW commander's aircraft, possibly the personal airplane of Brig Gen Darrell S Cramer, over Udorn in 1969. The squadron was known as 'Triple Nickel' and accounted for more MiGs than any other, but this airframe was serving with a different unit, the 435th TFS/8th TFW, when it shot down two MiG-17s on 6 November 1967 while crewed by Captain Darrell D Simmonds and 1st Lieutenant George H McKinney, Jr. Five Five Four survived the war and serves today with the Air Force Reserve at Dayton, Ohio
[*G R Zesinger*]

Right In the final days of the 1972 Linebacker campaign against North Vietnam, an F-4D Phantom from the 8th TFW 'Wolfpack' at Ubon Thailand flies formation with a KC-135 tanker while carrying a load of cluster bomb units (CBUs)
[*John Huggins*]

Above F-4E Phantom (67-0272), coded LC of the 481st TFS/366th TFW operating from Takhli, Thailand is seen in July 1972 with white-bordered canopy rails and a full warload, pushing towards Hanoi. Fighting became so heavy that F-4E squadrons were rushed to Southeast Asia on a temporary basis. The cannon introduced in the F-4E model never became a significant factor against MiGs, and most air-to-air kills were scored with Sidewinder missiles
[*John Huggins*]

Above right F-4D Phantom (66-7554), coded DO, of the 89th TFS/906th TFG, Air Force Reserve, stationed at Dayton, Ohio, shows off its twin MiG kills at Wright-Patterson AFB in August 1982
[*Charles W Arrington*]

Right The double MiG killer was nicknamed *City of Fairborn* (located near Dayton) and carries a commander's stripe and tail flash in addition to low-visibility national insignia
[*Charles W Arrington*]

Right District of Columbia Air National Guard's F-4D Phantom (66-7661) marked as a MiG killer is seen from the front on 8 March 1986 and makes a full afterburner takeoff on 15 March 1986 [*Joseph G Handelman*]

Below In recent years, the Marines at Andrews AFB, Maryland flew this Phantom without any distinctive marking on the airplane to denote its special status as a MiG killer. In April 1978, however, a MiG kill was still painted on the splitter vane of F-4N 150456, a former F-4B, coded MG-4 of the 'Hells Angels' of VMFA-321. The MiG-17 silhouetted inside the red star was shot down on 6 May 1972 when the Phantom belonged to VF-51 and was flown by Lieutenant Commander J Huston and Lieutenant K I Moore [*Joseph G Handelman*]

Foreign Phantoms

Arctic skies: Phantom FGR.2s of No 19 Sqn, Royal Air Force, take a close look a the spectacular scenery of Northern Norway during a deployment from their home base at Wildenrath, West Germany, in August 1982. XV430 (above) is pulling hard to find the right line as it turns into a fjord. The airplane is unarmed, but carries a blue Sparrow drill round to keep the CG (centre of gravity) within limits
[*Ian Black*]

Low and fast. The Barley Grey air defence
scheme (now standard on all RAF Phantoms
except the F-4Js of No 74 Sqn) is very
conspicuous in this type of environment. In 1978,
No 19 Sqn received the first RAF Phantom
sprayed in low-visibility grey
[*Ian Black*]

Interestingly, as late as 1982 this No 19 Sqn FGR.2 still retains RAF tactical Dark Green, Dark Sea Grey, and Light Aircraft Grey camouflage, but its underwing fuel tanks (each of 370 US gal capacity) are painted in air defence Barley Grey/Light Aircraft Grey. Because of financial contraints, it is rumored that the RAF were only allowed one set of wing tanks per aircraft and, except in the most dire emergency, jettisoning a pair of precious tanks is definitely *verboten*!
[*Ian Black*]

Since 1977, teamed with the Phantoms of 92 Sqn, No 19 has provided intercept and CAP (combat air patrol) cover for the British sector of West German airspace. They specialize in low-level air combat, exploiting the rapid supersonic urge of Rolls-Royce Spey turbofans (20,515 lb/9305 kg of thrust each in full 'burner), the enhanced detection capability of their digitized

Westinghouse AWG-12 radar, and an awesome array of weapons. Four Sky Flash medium-range radar guided air-to-air missiles, four AIM-9L infrared guided AAMs, and a rapid-fire centreline 20 mm cannon is firepower in spades. The basic vehicle may be getting a bit long in the tooth (according to insiders, if it isn't leaking fuel it must be a dead one!) but in skilled hands the current F-4M can still cut it with the best of them. Despite the advent of the Tornado F.3 air defence variant, the RAF is retaining its two Phantom squadrons in Germany until the Eurofighter is introduced in the late 1990s. XV472/'L' flies in contrasting Norwegian weather [*Ian Black*]

During 'Operation Corporate', the repossession of
the Falklands in 1982, a number of Phantoms
from No 29 Sqn were ferried to Wideawake
airfield on Ascension Island to prevent Argentine
surveillance of the military build-up and deal with
the possible threat of a pre-emptive strike by
special forces deployed from Hercules transports.
The air defence task on Ascension was originally
performed by Harriers, but these were desperately
needed by the naval task force. The day Stanley
Airport was recaptured, the Royal Engineers
began to prepare it for Phantoms, adding layers of
reinforced AM2 matting to produce a 6200 ft

(1890 m) runway. Flown by the commanding officer of No 29 Sqn, Wing Commander Ian MacFayden, and navigated by Squadron Leader Peter Simpson, the first Phantom into Stanley (XV468) arrived on 17 October 1982. MacFayden couldn't resist performing a victory roll over the airfield before landing. The 4,000-mile (6270-km) flight from Ascension took 8 hours and 45 minutes, and involved 7 in-flight refuellings from Victor K.2 tankers. The No 29 Sqn detachment at Stanley was subsequently redesignated No 23 Sqn (with the same aircraft) on 30 March 1983 and No 29 moved back to its home base at Coningsby in Lincolnshire. The loss of a full Phantom squadron to the South Atlantic denuded the UK's air defence capability to an unacceptable level and, as a direct result of the Falklands conflict, 15 F-4Js were purchased from US Navy stocks to form No 74 (Tiger) Sqn. **Left** FGR.2 XV423 takes shelter inside its Rubb hangar. No 23 Sqn moved to Mount Pleasant in 1985, the RAF's newest, most heavily defended, and most inappropriately named air base. **This page** On guard: Phantom XV420 waits for its crew in unusually fine weather [*Tristram Carter*]

No 23 Sqn is supported by Hercules C.1K tankers of No 1312 Flight—air-to-air refuelling forms an integral pary of operations. Formating on a lumbering Herk in a fast jet demands flying skill of the highest order, but the reward is a significant increase in the Phantom's radius of action. **Above** The missiles on the twin-launcher are Sidewinder AIM-9Ls; the lethality of this weapon was a decisive factor in maintaining British air superiority during the Falklands war [*Tristram Carter*]

The barren terrain of the Falkland Islands,
relieved by a patrolling FGR.2
[*Tristram Carter*]

Loaded for bear . . . fully armed Phantoms of 23
Sqn maintain the vigil to deter a repeat
performance of Argentina's invasion of 1 April
1982
[*Tristram Carter*]

Probe extended and ready to refuel, the nearest
Phantom prepares to slide into the pre-contact
position on the Hercules tanker. Each aircraft has
a Falklands badge on the nose, flanked by the
squadron's traditional red and blue bars
[*Tristram Carter*]

FGR.2 XV495 taxies out for takeoff. A late-production F-4M model, this airplane was originally delivered to No 6 Sqn at RAF Coningsby in September 1970. The F-4M is the only version of the Phantom equipped with an internal battery for engine starting—an obvious bonus when every second counts . . .
[*Tristram Carter*]

The Turkish Air Force is one of the least-
publicized users of the Phantom and these views
of its F-4E airplanes, 77-0295 (left), 77-0291
(above), and 77-0289 (overleaf) are a welcome
view of a NATO ally's equipment, taken at a
Turkish airfield on 14 November 1985
[*Robbie Shaw*]

Above F-4EJ Phantom (07-8430) of the JASDF's Hyakuri-based 305th Fighter Squadron, visiting Komatsu on 6 June 1982. This aircraft, in another variation of disruptive camouflage, crashed on 30 September 1982, and was written off
[*Hidelki Nagakubo*]

Overleaf F-4EJ Phantom (37-8309) of the JASDF's 301st Fighter Squadron at Hyakuri on 8 February 1978, wearing the paint scheme standard for the type until experimentation with colours began in the 1980s. This was one of a dozen Phantoms manufactured in St Louis before Mitsubishi took over production of the bulk of Japan's 140 airplanes
[*Masumi Wada*]